BRACKETIVITY
KIDS

32 Choices, One Winner!

By Cala Spinner

Andrews McMeel
PUBLISHING®

Andrews McMeel Publishing
a division of Andrews McMeel Universal
1130 Walnut Street, Kansas City, Missouri 64106

www.andrewsmcmeel.com

23 24 25 26 27 RLP 10 9 8 7 6 5 4 3 2 1

ISBN: 978-1-5248-7740-8

ATTENTION: SCHOOLS AND BUSINESSES

Andrews McMeel books are available at quantity discounts with bulk purchase for educational, business, or sales promotional use. For information, please e-mail the Andrews McMeel Publishing Special Sales Department: sales@amuniversal.com.

BRACKETIVITY
KIDS

What's your favorite flavor of ice cream—rocky road or vanilla? Cookie dough or strawberry? Chocolate or pistachio?

In your hand is a very special book. Within these pages, you'll be able to pick your favorite "thing" in each category. But it's not just a "pick and go" situation—you'll have to fill in each bracket to determine your winner! These brackets are called **BRACKETIVITIES**!

Think about each answer carefully because it determines your next round of **bracketivities**. Or go with your gut feeling—really, there's no wrong answer! And at the end of the book, you'll even get to make your own **bracketivities** to share with family and friends.

So, grab a pen, pencil, or crayon (but probably not marker—those pesky tools can bleed through!), and get going. Just remember—have fun!

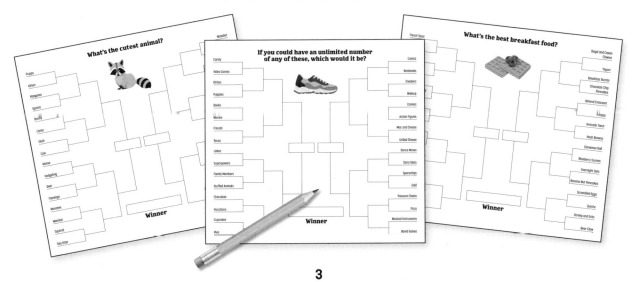

What's the best flavor of ice cream?

BRACKETIVITY EXAMPLE

Here's an example **bracketivity** that's filled out. It's what your author would pick. Don't worry—if you disagree, you'll get to fill out your own **bracketivity** on the next page.

Chocolate
Chocolate
Cookie Dough
Chocolate
Peanut Butter
Peanut Butter
Raspberry

Pistachio

Pistachio
Pistachio
Rocky Road
Pistachio
Bubble Gum
Strawberry
Strawberry

Salted Caramel
Birthday Cake
Birthday Cake
Cookies and Cream
Cookies and Cream
Cookies and Cream
Mango

Cookies and Cream

Coconut
Coconut
Lemon Sorbet
Vanilla
Mint Chocolate Chip
Vanilla
Vanilla

Cotton Candy
Cotton Candy
Cotton Candy
Coffee
Cotton Candy
Butter Pecan
Chocolate Chip
Chocolate Chip

Cheesecake

Neapolitan
Neapolitan
Butterscotch
Neapolitan
Cheesecake
Cherry
Cheesecake
Cheesecake

Watermelon
Praline
Praline
Praline
Eggnog
Banana Swirl
Banana Swirl

Praline

Rum Raisin
Tutti Frutti
Tutti Frutti
Maple Walnut
Key Lime Pie
Maple Walnut
Maple Walnut

Cookies and Cream — **Cheesecake**

Cheesecake
Winner

4

What's the best flavor of ice cream?

Chocolate

Cookie Dough

Peanut Butter

Raspberry

Pistachio

Rocky Road

Bubble Gum

Strawberry

Salted Caramel

Birthday Cake

Cookies and Cream

Mango

Coconut

Lemon Sorbet

Mint Chocolate Chip

Vanilla

Winner

Cotton Candy

Coffee

Butter Pecan

Chocolate Chip

Neapolitan

Butterscotch

Cherry

Cheesecake

Watermelon

Praline

Eggnog

Banana Swirl

Rum Raisin

Tutti Frutti

Key Lime Pie

Maple Walnut

What's the best place for a school field trip?

Art Museum

Botanical Gardens

TV Station

Movie Theater

Planetarium

Opera

Fish Hatchery

Pumpkin Patch

National Park

Fire Station

Theme Park

Zoo

Recycling Center

Greenhouse

Roller Skating Rink

Vegetable Farm

Aquarium

Apple Orchard

Circus

Radio Station

Lumber Mill

Beach

Boat Tour

Library

Haunted House

Water Park

Ice-Skating Rink

Government Office

Police Station

Air Show

Baseball Game

Military Base

Winner

What's the best breakfast food?

French Toast

Waffles

Cheese Omelet

Cereal

English Muffin

Sausage, Egg, and Cheese Sandwich

Banana Bread

Cheese Danish

Cranberry Muffin

Maple Doughnut

Eggs Over Easy

Smoothie

Granola

Toaster Strudel

Bacon

Biscuits and Gravy

Bagel and Cream Cheese

Yogurt

Breakfast Burrito

Chocolate Chip Pancakes

Almond Croissant

Frittata

Avocado Toast

Hash Browns

Cinnamon Roll

Blueberry Scones

Overnight Oats

Banana Nut Pancakes

Scrambled Eggs

Quiche

Shrimp and Grits

Bear Claw

Winner

Of these, which is your dream job?

Actor

Illustrator

Taxi Driver

Salesperson

Nurse

Graphic Designer

Pet Groomer

Airplane Pilot

Scientist

Hairdresser

Firefighter

Professional Athlete

Therapist

Teacher

Pediatrician

Writer

Lawyer

Bakery Owner

Postal Service

Dentist

Realtor

Race Car Driver

Video Game Developer

Business Owner

Surgeon

Chef

Model

Musician

Truck Driver

Architect

Film Director

Book Editor

Winner

Which American city would you most like to visit?

New York, NY

Chicago, IL

Kansas City, MO

Houston, TX

Denver, CO

Phoenix, AZ

Savannah, GA

Raleigh, NC

Milwaukee, WI

Seattle, WA

San Diego, CA

New Orleans, LA

Portland, ME

St. Louis, MO

Washington, DC

Nashville, TN

San Francisco, CA

Dallas, TX

Miami, FL

Los Angeles, CA

Portland, OR

Detroit, MI

Atlanta, GA

Austin, TX

Honolulu, HI

Anchorage, AK

Boston, MA

Salt Lake City, UT

Orlando, FL

Las Vegas, NV

Sacramento, CA

Tulsa, OK

Winner

What's the best flower?

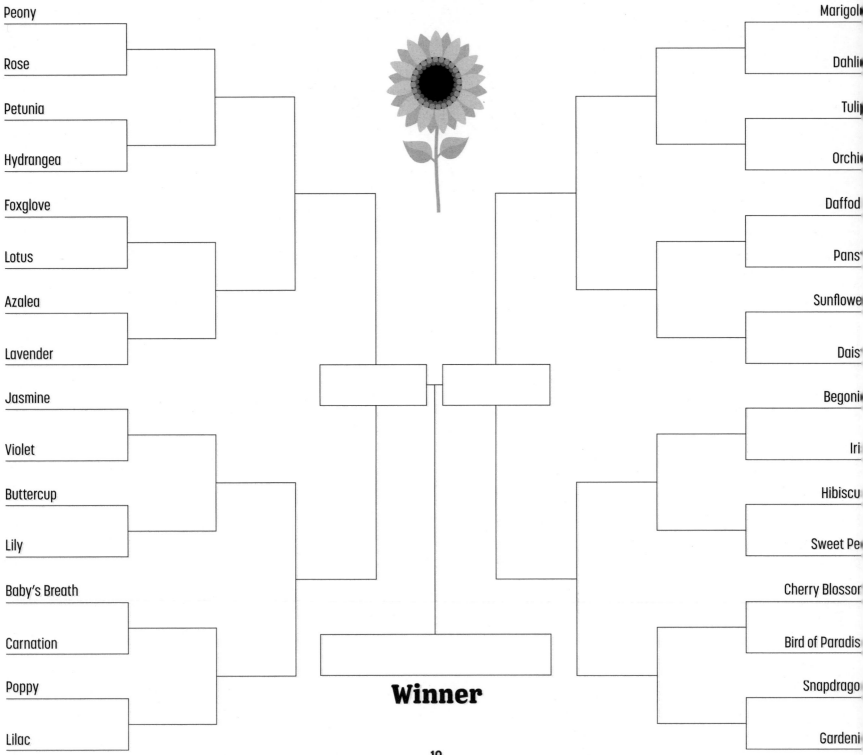

Peony

Rose

Petunia

Hydrangea

Foxglove

Lotus

Azalea

Lavender

Jasmine

Violet

Buttercup

Lily

Baby's Breath

Carnation

Poppy

Lilac

Marigold

Dahlia

Tulip

Orchid

Daffodil

Pansy

Sunflower

Daisy

Begonia

Iris

Hibiscus

Sweet Pea

Cherry Blossom

Bird of Paradise

Snapdragon

Gardenia

Winner

Imagine you have a time machine!
Who would you most want to meet?

Nelson Mandela

William Shakespeare

John Lennon

Amelia Earhart

Pablo Picasso

Aristotle

Roald Dahl

King Tutankhamun

George Washington

Babe Ruth

Martin Luther King Jr.

Audrey Hepburn

Cleopatra

Edgar Allan Poe

Elvis Presley

Anne Frank

Alexander the Great

Marilyn Monroe

Mahatma Gandhi

Leonardo da Vinci

Abraham Lincoln

Rosa Parks

Bob Marley

Joe DiMaggio

Walt Disney

Muhammad Ali

Thomas Edison

Princess Diana

Carrie Fisher

Benjamin Franklin

Neil Armstrong

Jimi Hendrix

Winner

Write in your own:

With the following prompt, fill in your own bracketivity!

What are your favorite stores to shop at?
Write them in the 32 choices on the sides.
Then, find out which one would win!

Winner

What's the best costume?

Witch

Baby Shark

Video Game Character

Park Ranger

Fairy

Royalty

Superhero

Knight

Nurse

Zombie

Ghost

Astronaut

Hippie

Angel

Prisoner

Clown

Genie

Vampire

Unicorn

Kitty

Police Officer

Skeleton

Little Red Riding Hood

Rapunzel

Scarecrow

Doctor

Robot

Dragon

Circus Master

Mermaid

Dinosaur

Supervillain

Winner

Of these, which food is your LEAST favorite?

Brussels Sprouts

Avocado

Pistachio

Dark Chocolate

Butternut Squash

Eggs

Hot Sauce

Peas

Fish

Cauliflower

Peaches

Pumpkin Pie

Asparagus

Stale Bread

Mushrooms

Spinach

Shrimp

Chicken

Lunch Meat

Green Beans

Cottage Cheese

Cabbage

Olives

Candy Corn

Tomatoes

Beets

Licorice

Eggplant

Bleu Cheese

Tofu

Oysters

Raisins

Winner

What's the best way to spend a rainy day?

Play Video Games

Draw

Go Bowling

Play Hide-and-Seek

Do a Science Experiment

Call a Friend

Listen to a Podcast

Make a Model Kit

Play Dress-Up

Make Jewelry

Build a Couch Fort

Catch Up on Homework

Cook Something New

Clean Your Room

Watch TV

Listen to Music

Winner

Practice a Musical Instrument

Read a Book

Complete a Puzzle

Play with a Pet

Bake a Cake

Paint

Scavenger Hunt

Dance

Make Slime

Have a Movie Marathon

Go to a Museum

Play Cards

Write a Story

Host a Tea Party

Go Indoor Roller-Skating

Play a Board Game

What's the cutest animal?

Puppy

Kitten

Kangaroo

Iguana

Bunny

Llama

Sloth

Cow

Moose

Hedgehog

Deer

Flamingo

Manatee

Meerkat

Squirrel

Sea Otter

Wombat

Goldfish

Red Panda

Ferret

Fox

Elephant

Parakeet

Hippo

Giraffe

Pony

Goat

Skunk

Duck

Raccoon

Seal

Platypus

Winner

If you could have an unlimited number of any of these, which would it be?

Candy

Video Games

Kitties

Puppies

Books

Movies

Friends

Tacos

Jokes

Superpowers

Family Members

Stuffed Animals

Chocolate

Vacations

Cupcakes

Pies

Comics

Notebooks

Sneakers

Makeup

Cookies

Action Figures

Mac and Cheese

Grilled Cheese

Dance Moves

Story Ideas

Spaceships

Gold

Treasure Chests

Pizza

Musical Instruments

Board Games

Winner

What's your favorite emoji?

You'll have to draw this one out!

Winner

Of these, who is your favorite musician or group?

Taylor Swift

Dua Lipa

Beyoncé

Billie Eilish

Rihanna

Camila Cabello

Doja Cat

Dolly Parton

Ariana Grande

Shawn Mendes

BTS

Bruno Mars

The Beatles

Lady Gaga

The Weeknd

Olivia Rodrigo

Justin Bieber

Elvis

Harry Styles

Post Malone

The Rolling Stones

Ed Sheeran

Katy Perry

Adele

Alicia Keys

Selena Gomez

Drake

Eminem

Red Hot Chili Peppers

Green Day

Miley Cyrus

BLACKPINK

music FESTIVAL
00123456
5,00$ CITY STADIUM | JUNE 21ST
SEC 02 ROW 10 SEAT 35
ADMIT ONE

Winner

Imagine you're at the dog park!
Which dog breed do you most want to pet?

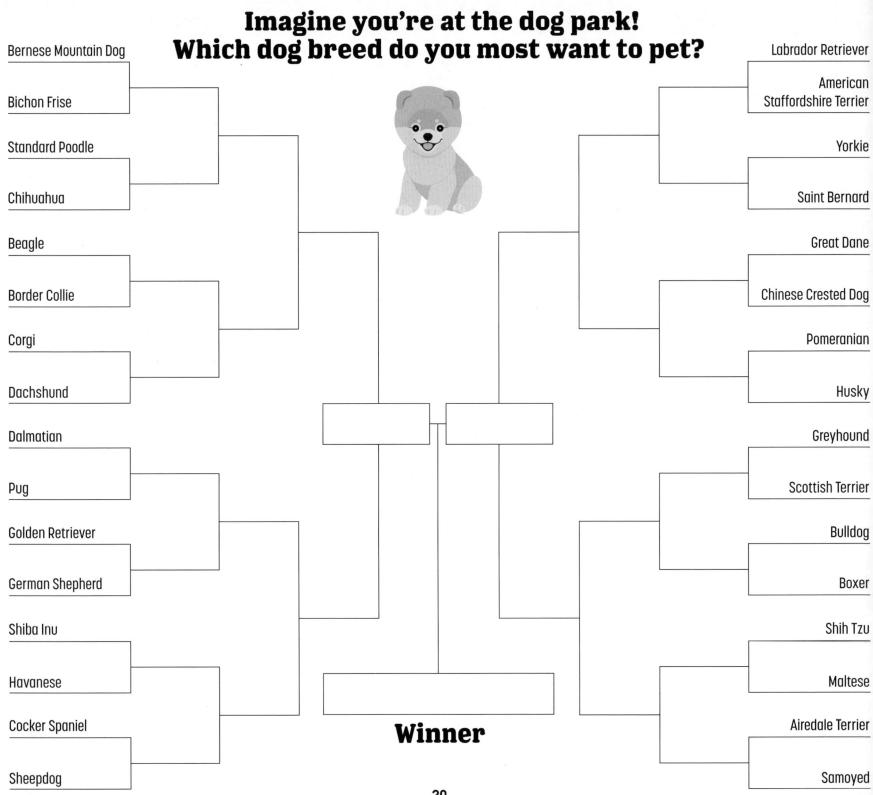

Bernese Mountain Dog

Bichon Frise

Standard Poodle

Chihuahua

Beagle

Border Collie

Corgi

Dachshund

Dalmatian

Pug

Golden Retriever

German Shepherd

Shiba Inu

Havanese

Cocker Spaniel

Sheepdog

Labrador Retriever

American Staffordshire Terrier

Yorkie

Saint Bernard

Great Dane

Chinese Crested Dog

Pomeranian

Husky

Greyhound

Scottish Terrier

Bulldog

Boxer

Shih Tzu

Maltese

Airedale Terrier

Samoyed

Winner

A "bucket list" is a list of things someone wants to do in life.

Among these choices, what do you most want to do?

Compete in the Olympics

Swim in Every Ocean

Learn How to Ski

Take a Hot-Air Balloon Ride

See the Egyptian Pyramids

Go Whitewater Rafting

Kayak with Whales

Go on an African Safari

Rescue an Animal

Watch a Volcano Erupt

Visit Stonehenge

Volunteer for a Homeless Shelter

See a Broadway Musical

Go Skydiving

Go to all the Disney Theme Parks

Ride in a Gondola

Visit Dracula's Castle

Get Married

Visit all Seven Wonders of the Modern World

Backpack across Europe

Go to College

Travel through the Amazon Rainforest

Climb Mt. Everest

Go Mountain Biking

Become a Billionaire

Visit the Grand Canyon

Watch a Meteor Shower

Become a Blood Donor

Go to the Super Bowl

Act in a Movie

Enter an Eating Contest

Dance in the Rain

Winner

Write in your own:

With the following prompt, fill in your own bracketivity!

Think about all your favorite movie or TV characters. Write them in the 32 choices on the sides. Then, find out which one would win!

Winner

Which city in Europe would you most like to visit?

Rome, Italy

Copenhagen, Denmark

Milan, Italy

Reykjavík, Iceland

Berlin, Germany

Santorini, Greece

Prague,
Czech Republic

Geneva, Switzerland

Amsterdam,
The Netherlands

Venice, Italy

Madrid, Spain

Edinburgh, Scotland

Moscow, Russia

Vienna, Austria

Stockholm, Sweden

Florence, Italy

Brussels, Belgium

Athens, Greece

Istanbul, Turkey

Budapest, Hungary

Barcelona, Spain

Warsaw, Poland

Lisbon, Portugal

Dublin, Ireland

Paris, France

Oslo, Norway

Saint Petersburg,
Russia

Bruges, Belgium

Naples, Italy

Bucharest, Romania

London, England

Palermo, Italy

Winner

Which country would you most like to visit?

China

France

Switzerland

South Africa

Japan

India

Pakistan

Malaysia

Canada

Brazil

Colombia

Australia

Egypt

Singapore

Germany

Madagascar

Romania

United Arab Emirates

Argentina

Italy

Korea

Turkey

Thailand

Spain

New Zealand

Panama

Sweden

Netherlands

Hong Kong

Austria

Mexico

United Kingdom

Winner

What's your favorite fruit?

Apple

Strawberry

Banana

Clementine

Peach

Cherry

Blueberry

Tangerine

Kiwi

Grapefruit

Pear

Cranberry

Watermelon

Nectarine

Apricot

Pomegranate

Lime

Lemon

Blackberry

Honeydew Melon

Pineapple

Cantaloupe

Dates

Mango

Plum

Orange

Raspberry

Coconut

Grapes

Avocado

Tomato

Papaya

Winner

What's the best animated film?

Encanto

Hotel Transylvania

Mulan

How to Train Your Dragon

Finding Nemo

Shrek

Kung Fu Panda

Frozen

The Little Mermaid

Inside Out

Brave

Despicable Me

Tangled

Raya and the Last Dragon

Coco

The Lion King

Moana

Spider-Man: Into the Spider-Verse

The Incredibles

Big Hero 6

Zootopia

Ratatouille

Toy Story

Puss in Boots

Trolls

Cars

A Bug's Life

Sleeping Beauty

Snow White

Cinderella

Alice in Wonderland

Winnie the Pooh

Winner

Which animal would win in a fight?

Gorilla

Cheetah

Polar Bear

Blue Whale

Horse

Dung Beetle

Panther

Spider

Rhino

Zebra

Badger

Wolverine

Scorpion

Python

Eagle

Tiger

Hyena

Musk Ox

Elephant

Poisonous Frog

Mountain Lion

Cobra

Buffalo

Wolf

Hawk

Grizzly Bear

Anaconda

Crocodile

Hippopotamus

Jaguar

Boar

Camel

Winner

What's the best school lunch?

Macaroni and Cheese

Shepherd's Pie

Chicken Nuggets

Jamaican Beef Patty

Cheese Pizza

Beef Tacos

Chicken and Cheese Taquitos

Salad

Falafel Wraps

Peanut Butter and Jelly Sandwich

Turkey, Ham, and Cheese Melt

Bean and Cheese Burrito

Cheeseburger

Chicken Teriyaki

Nachos

Turkey and Cheese Sub

Mexican Pizza

Spaghetti and Red Sauce

Hot Dog

Egg Salad Sandwich

Tuna Salad Sandwich

Chili

Mini Corn Dogs

Fajitas

Mini Quesadillas

Turkey Burger

Fish Sticks

Sloppy Joes

Broccoli Cheddar Potato Bowl

BBQ Chicken and Rice

Vegetable Burger

Ramen

Winner

Which sport/activity would you most like to play or partake in?

Ice Skating

Soccer

Football

Sailing

Cheerleading

Hockey

Horse-Back Riding

Tennis

Golf

Bowling

Archery

Lacrosse

Swimming

Fencing

Baseball

Badminton

Cross-Country

Roller-Skating

Cricket

Karate

Volleyball

Wrestling

Rugby

Gymnastics

Basketball

Surfing

Tae Kwon Do

Rowing

Kickboxing

Weightlifting

Softball

Chess

Winner

Out of these options, what's your favorite color?

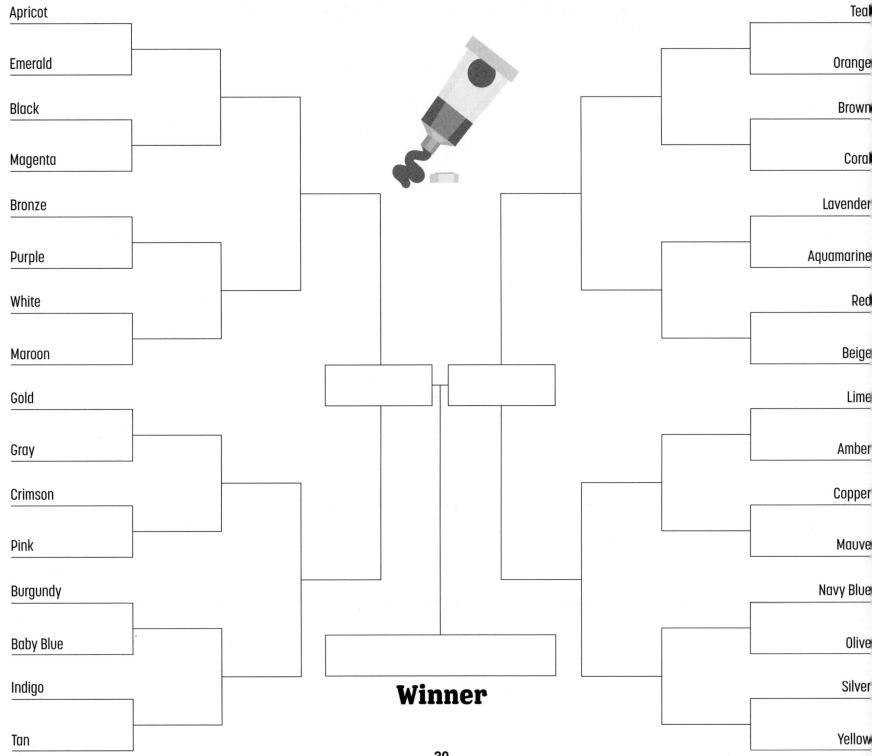

Apricot

Emerald

Black

Magenta

Bronze

Purple

White

Maroon

Gold

Gray

Crimson

Pink

Burgundy

Baby Blue

Indigo

Tan

Teal

Orange

Brown

Coral

Lavender

Aquamarine

Red

Beige

Lime

Amber

Copper

Mauve

Navy Blue

Olive

Silver

Yellow

Winner

Out of these options, what's your LEAST favorite color?

(Hint: It's like the last page but in reverse!)

Apricot

Emerald

Black

Magenta

Bronze

Purple

White

Maroon

Gold

Gray

Crimson

Pink

Burgundy

Baby Blue

Indigo

Tan

Teal

Orange

Brown

Coral

Lavender

Aquamarine

Red

Beige

Lime

Amber

Copper

Mauve

Navy Blue

Olive

Silver

Yellow

Winner

Write in your own:

With the following prompt, fill in your own bracketivity!

Do you have any nicknames? Do you WISH you had any nicknames? Write them in the 32 choices on the sides. Then, find out which one you would most like to be called!

HELLO MY NAME IS Isabella

HELLO MY NAME IS Jayden

Winner

Which video game is your favorite?

LEVEL UP

Animal Crossing

Mario Kart

Rocket League

Hello Neighbor

Fortnite

Pokémon

Piggy

Stardew Valley

Bendy and the Ink Machine

Five Nights at Freddy's

Among Us

Tomb Raider

Roblox

The Legend of Zelda: Breath of the Wild

Pac-Man

Tetris

Just Dance

Super Smash Bros.

Minecraft

Sonic the Hedgehog

The Sims

Untitled Goose Game

Cuphead

Kingdom Hearts

Kirby

Overwatch

Ratchet & Clank

Splatoon

Life Is Strange

Spider-Man

World of Warcraft

Spyro

Winner

What's the best candy?

Candy Corn

Smarties

Skittles

M&Ms

Hershey Kisses

Tootsie Rolls

Black Licorice

Peanut Butter Cups

Snickers

Twix

Kit Kat

Milk Duds

Sour Patch Kids

Butterfinger

Saltwater Taffy

Chupa Chups

Winner

Starburst

Swedish Fish

Jolly Ranchers

Gummy Bears

Sweet Tarts

Peach Rings

Twizzlers

Chocolate Mints

Hot Tamales

Chocolate-Covered Raisins

Milky Way

Almond Joy

Peanut M&Ms

Circus Peanuts

Whoppers

Homemade Candy

Which classic movie could you watch again and again?

Home Alone

Harry Potter and the Sorcerer's Stone

Mary Poppins

The Wizard of Oz

Grease

Singin' in the Rain

Elf

Matilda

The Sandlot

Honey, I Shrunk the Kids

Back to the Future

Jumanji

The Karate Kid

Annie

The NeverEnding Story

Star Wars

Winner

The Muppet Movie

The Sound of Music

Miracle on 34th Street

E.T. the Extra-Terrestrial

Willy Wonka & the Chocolate Factory

The Parent Trap

Indiana Jones and the Raiders of the Lost Ark

Jurassic Park

Babe

Pee-wee's Big Adventure

The Princess Bride

The Goonies

The Chronicles of Narnia: The Lion, the Witch and the Wardrobe

School of Rock

Casper

Hocus Pocus

Which pet would you most want to take care of?

(But maybe stick with the more traditional pets for real life!)

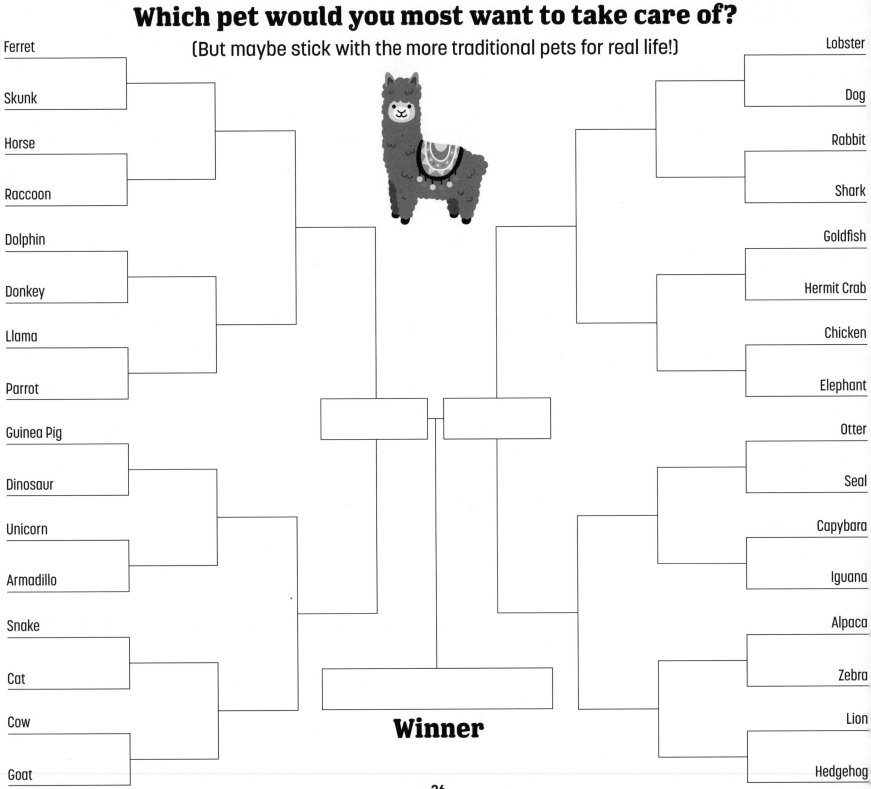

Ferret

Skunk

Horse

Raccoon

Dolphin

Donkey

Llama

Parrot

Guinea Pig

Dinosaur

Unicorn

Armadillo

Snake

Cat

Cow

Goat

Lobster

Dog

Rabbit

Shark

Goldfish

Hermit Crab

Chicken

Elephant

Otter

Seal

Capybara

Iguana

Alpaca

Zebra

Lion

Hedgehog

Winner

What's the creepiest insect?

Fire Ants

Bumblebees

Cockroaches

Wasps

Dung Beetles

Ladybugs

Fireflies

Scarab Beetles

Grasshoppers

Moths

Fleas

Crickets

Dragonflies

Fruit Flies

Water Scorpions

Cicadas

Water Bugs

Stink Bugs

Silverfish

Weevils

Biting Lice

Locusts

Butterflies

Stick Insects

Earwigs

Bed Bugs

Termites

Mosquitoes

Gnats

Hornets

Caterpillars

Mealworms

Winner

You have unlimited appetizers at your favorite restaurant!

What are you picking?

Nachos

Mozzarella Sticks

Chips and Salsa

Buffalo Chicken Dip

Sliders

Shrimp Cocktail

Pigs in a Blanket

Poutine

Tater Tots

Cauliflower Wings

Chicken Nuggets

Spinach Artichoke Dip

Stuffed Mushrooms

Deviled Eggs

Chips and Guacamole

Potato Skins

Onion Rings

Chile Con Queso

Mac and Cheese Bites

Mini Quesadillas

Sweet Potato Fries

Tomato Soup

Jalapeño Poppers

Vegetables and Hummus

Chicken Taquitos

Stuffed Peppers

Coconut Shrimp

Blue Cheese Dip

Baked Brie

Empanadas

Pizza Rolls

Pork Dumplings

Winner

What book or series would you most want to check out from the library?

The Secret Garden

The Lion, the Witch, and the Wardrobe

Charlie and the Chocolate Factory

Charlotte's Web

Where the Wild Things Are

Harry Potter and the Sorcerer's Stone

The Phantom Tollbooth

The Little Prince

The Baby-Sitters Club

Little Women

The Great Adventures of Sherlock Holmes

A Wrinkle in Time

James and the Giant Peach

Anne of Green Gables

Wonder

Guts

Diary of a Wimpy Kid

Dog Man

Number the Stars

The Jungle Book

Little House on the Prairie

Ramona

Alice's Adventures in Wonderland

Matilda

The Hobbit

Nancy Drew

The Lorax

Percy Jackson & the Olympians: The Lightning Thief

Holes

Wings of Fire

Tales of a Fourth Grade Nothing

Big Nate

Winner

What's your favorite vegetable or legume?

Red Peppers

Artichokes

Green Cabbage

Cauliflower

Mushrooms

Kale

Bok Choy

Asparagus

Broccoli

Sweetcorn

Celery

Onions

Broccoli Rabe

Beets

Arugula

Carrots

Collard Greens

Brussels Sprouts

Sweet Peas

Green Peppers

Radishes

Chives

Potatoes

Green Beans

Sweet Potatoes

Okra

Spinach

Yellow Peppers

Red Cabbage

Turnips

Radicchio

Swiss Chard

Winner

What's your favorite school subject?

Geography

French

Music

Health

Journalism

Astronomy

Computer Science

Art History

Drama

German

Spanish

World History

Design

Social Studies

Drama

Philosophy

Physical Education

Environmental Science

Sculpture

English

Psychology

Cooking

American History

Chemistry

Painting

Biology

Economics

Religion

American Sign Language

Creative Writing

Physics

Algebra

Winner

Write in your own:

With the following prompt, fill in your own bracketivity!

Think about all the names you'd give a new puppy. Write them in the 32 choices on the sides. Then, find out which one would win!

Winner

What's your favorite kind of cheese?

Brie

Camembert

Gruyère

Halloumi

Gouda

Feta

Blue

Fontina

Raclette

String Cheese

Cotija

Stilton

Provolone

Ricotta

Pecorino Romano

Muenster

Mozzarella

American

Paneer

Havarti

Soy

Cottage Cheese

Burrata

Gorgonzola

Cheddar

Manchego

Labneh

Cream Cheese

Monterey Jack

Asiago

Nacho Cheese

Parmesan

Winner

What's the best flavor of cupcake?

Red Velvet

Strawberry Shortcake

Lemon Custard

Carrot Cake

Crème Brûlée

Mocha Espresso

Peanut Butter & Jelly

Chocolate

Vanilla Buttercream

Tiramisu

Peppermint Mocha

Blueberry

Maple Bacon

Strawberry

Chocolate Hazelnut

Peaches and Cream

Banana Split

Dulce de Leche

Toffee

Marble

Coconut Crumble

Confetti

Banana Pudding

Cinnamon

Salted Caramel

Boston Cream

Chocolate Peanut Butter

Cotton Candy

Snickerdoodle

Black Forest

Rainbow Sprinkles

Passionfruit

Winner

What's the best pizza topping?

Pepperoni

Jalapeños

Mushrooms

Tomatoes

Fresh Basil

Black Olives

Balsamic Glaze

Roasted Garlic

Chicken

Pineapple

Anchovies

Artichokes

Pesto

Ricotta

Roasted Red Peppers

Bacon

Fresh Mozzarella

Sausage

Green Peppers

Canadian Bacon

Meatballs

Parmesan

BBQ Sauce

Spinach

Sun-Dried Tomatoes

Salami

Caramelized Onions

Chorizo

Pulled Pork

Alfredo Sauce

Fresh Garlic

Buffalo Sauce

Winner

What's the scariest-looking animal?

Wolverine

Bat

Anglerfish

Shark

Naked Mole-Rat

Blobfish

Manta Ray

Cheetah

Piranha

Lion

Tarantula

Vulture

Falcon

Gorilla

Grizzly Bear

Anaconda

Alligator

Boar

Wildebeest

Scorpion

Hawk

Tapeworm

Centipede

Orca

Hyena

Wolf

Swordfish

Spider Monkey

Rhino

Toad

Giant Squid

Sea Urchin

Winner

Which mythical creature would you most like to meet?

Unicorn

Mermaid

Leprechaun

Loch Ness Monster

Hippogriff

Phoenix

Cyclops

Bogeyman

Goblin

Fairy

Bigfoot

Gorgon

Ogre

Gnome

Minotaur

Chimera

Sphinx

Yeti

Hydra

Zombie

Werewolf

Vampire

Banshee

Basilisk

Dragon

Centaur

Troll

Winged Lion

Pixie

Ghoul

Manticore

Narwhal

Winner

What's the best thing to do on a hot summer day?

Play Soccer

Go to the Beach

Watch a
Baseball Game

Have a
Scavenger Hunt

Go to the Zoo

Build a Tree House

Go to a Water Park

Climb a Tree

Blow Bubbles

Take a Bike Ride

Go Camping

Have a Picnic

Go for a Walk

Open a
Lemonade Stand

Go Horseback Riding

Go to a Carnival

Swim in a Pool

Eat Ice Cream

Plant a Garden

Go Sailing

Play Board Games

Go to a Barbecue

Build a Bird House

Play Mini Golf

Go to a Theme Park

Fly a Kite

Jump on a Trampoline

Have a Water
Balloon Fight

Go Fishing

Draw with
Sidewalk Chalk

Visit an Outdoor Mall

Go Hiking

Winner

It's dessert time! Which dessert wins?

Hot Fudge Sundae

Apple Pie

Peach Cobbler

Funnel Cake

Chocolate Chip Cookie

Doughnut

Brownie

Whoopie Pie

Beignet

Chocolate Fondue

Fruit Salad

Cupcake

Banana Pudding

Tiramisu

Mochi

Ice Cream Cake

Winner

Molten Lava Cake

Boston Cream Pie

Cheesecake

Key Lime Pie

Cinnamon Roll

Banana Bread

Blueberry Muffin

Baked Apple

Lemon Cake

Black and White Cookie

Chocolate Babka

Candied Apples

Butterscotch Pudding

Strawberry Shortcake

Apple Crisp

Angel Food Cake

If you had a superpower, what would you want it to be?

Super Speed

Mind Reading

Web Shooters

X-Ray Vision

Telekinesis

Invisibility

Super Hearing

Hypnosis

Smoke Generation

Ability to Talk to Animals

Projection

Sonic Scream

Aquatic Breathing

Poison Immunity

Super Vision

Agility

Night Vision

Ability to Brew Potions

Be in Two Places at Once

Memory Manipulation

Vocal Mind Control

Healing

Camouflage

Shapeshifting

Reality Warping

Ability to Wield Fire

Speed Swimming

Time Travel

Teleportation

Flight

Elasticity

Spell Casting

Winner

What birthday party idea sounds the most fun?

Mini Golf

Roller-Skating

Paintball

Laser Tag

Painting Pottery

Going to a Movie

Sleepover

Picnic

Going to a Restaurant

Alpaca Farm

Going on a Trip

Riding in a Limousine

Escape Room

Bowling

Going to a Spa

Trampoline Park

Pizza-Making Class

Outdoor Barbecue

Science Museum

Art Museum

Taking an Art Class

Water Park

Theme Park

Arcade

Skiing Resort

Aquarium

Zoo

Ice-Skating

Going to the Beach

Having Fun at Home

Cupcake Decorating

Karaoke

Winner

Write in your own:

With the following prompt, fill in your own bracketivity!

Imagine you're going to space. Think about all the things you're excited to do in space and write them in the 32 choices on the sides. Then, find out which one would win!

Winner

What's the best drink?

Chocolate Milkshake

Iced Tea

Water

Soda

Orange Juice

Fruit Punch

Lemonade

Eggnog

Fruit Smoothie

Shirley Temple

Protein Drink

Milk

Seltzer

Coconut Water

Kombucha

Energy Drink

Green Tea

Watermelon Juice

Italian Soda

Strawberry Lemonade

Mango Slushie

Pomegranate Juice

Chocolate Milk

Vanilla Milkshake

Ginger Ale

Root Beer

Hot Chocolate

Peppermint Mocha

Drinkable Yogurt

Grape Juice

Cranberry Juice

Apple Cider

Winner

Which cookie would you most like to eat?

Oatmeal Raisin

Peanut Butter

Shortbread

Gingerbread

Chocolate Chip

Sugar

Snickerdoodle

Whoopie Pie

White Chocolate
Macadamia Nut

Gingersnap

Macaroon

Butter Pecan

Crinkle

Molasses

Blueberry

Thumbprint

Mexican Wedding

Lemon Drop

Rainbow

Fudge

Pinwheel

Red Velvet

Fortune Cookie

Pumpkin Spice

Wafer

Salted Pretzel

S'mores

Biscotti

Maple Leaf Cream

Pizzelle

Meringue

Lemon Cream

Winner

Now it's your turn!

You're a pro at bracketivities. Turn the page and make your own.
You can also use this page to jot down any notes you have.

Winner

Winner

Winner

Winner

Winner

Winner

Winner

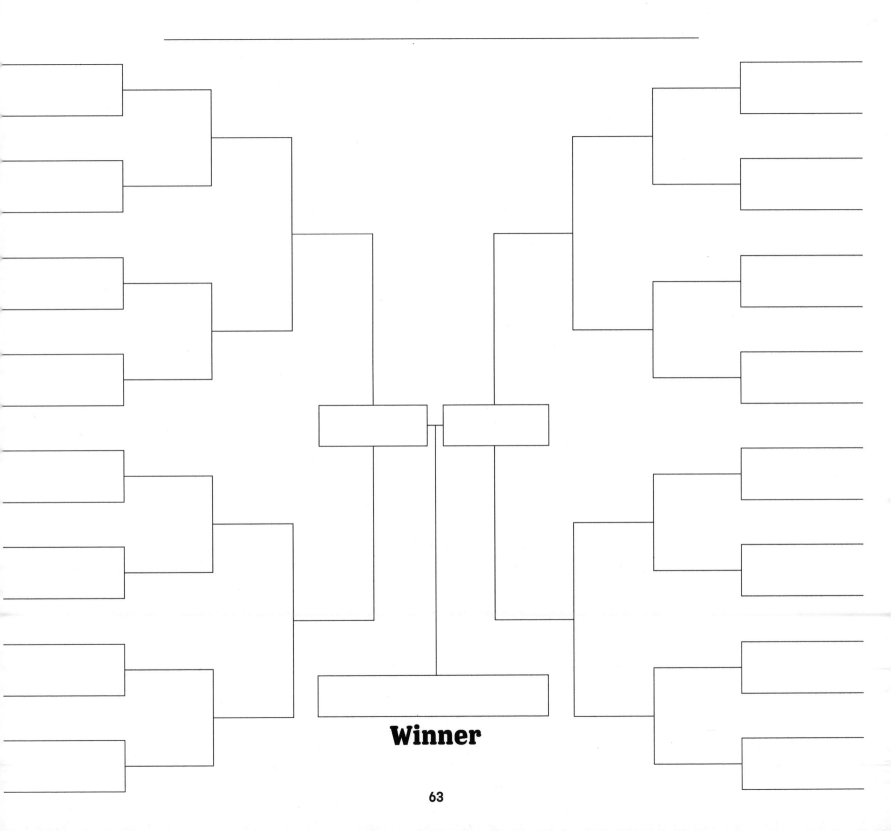

Winner

Winner